To:

From:

me and my DAD

Compiled and Illustrated by Stuart Hample

———————— ★ ————————

WORKMAN PUBLISHING, NEW YORK

Library of Congress Cataloging-in Publication Data

Me and my dad / compiled and illustrated by Stuart Hample.
p. cm.
ISBN 0-7611-1574-9
1. Fathers. 2. Children's writings. I. Hample, Stuart E.
HQ756.M4 1999
306.874'2—dc21 99-21249
CIP

Cover and interior design by Lisa Hollander and Kristen M. Nobles

Workman books are available at special discounts when purchased in bulk
for premiums and sales promotions as well as for fund-raising or educational use.
Special editions or book excerpts can also be created to specification.
For details, contact the Special Sales Director at the address below.

Workman Publishing Company, Inc.
708 Broadway
New York, NY 10003-9555

Printed in Mexico

First printing April 1999
10 9 8 7 6 5 4 3 2

To Joe, Henry, Martha, and Zack,
without whom I wouldn't be a dad.
And for Naomi, who helped make
me a better one.

A+

This is to acknowledge (in alphabetical order) the helping hands of Lois Blume, Joyce Blyn, Frank Buffone, Rose Cooper, Rita DeBrito, Keven Fittinghoff, Janet Harris and her intrepid troops, Rachel Landau, Lindsay MacGregor, Eric Marshall (or whatever his name is), Janis McCarty, Ellen Morgenstern, Kristen and Robin Nobles, Steve Plaut, Stanley Seidman, Lisa Solomon, the lion-hearted Ruth Sullivan, and some marvelous kids. Finally, for transmogrifying me from a cartoonist into an illustrator—and bringing color into my life—an extra kiss to Lisa Hollander.

CONTENTS

INTRODUCTION

——— ✦ ———

Although family structures have altered considerably over the last generation or so, it remains one of the immutable facts of life that the interactions between kids and fathers give off touching—and amusing—sparks.

Today's dad, who spends more time caring for his children than fathers of the past, seeks not only to provide, protect and love, but also to teach and nurture, as well as share child-rearing chores with his mate (who often holds down her own full-time job).

But despite his best efforts, no dad is always A-plus in the eyes of his children. So while many of the testimonies herein are, of course, paeans to dads, others descend the marking scale to an occasional C-minus due to some recondite pecadillo of which the allegedly erring father is totally unaware.

Nonetheless, kids boldly offer these warts-and-all bulletins without fear of reprisals, for they know in their stout little hearts that there's barely a dad nowadays (no matter how enlightened) who isn't putty in the hands of his offspring.

Full of surprises and rueful truths, flavored with a blend of love, laughter, and honesty, here are touching observations from kids—ages 7 to 11—(with grammatical and spelling lapses intact) about the male half of the parenting team.

—Stuart Hample (father of 4)

GENERAL OBSERVATIONS

My dad likes to read Good Night Moon to me because he said it's his favorite book. And I snuggle down and cuddle under the covers with my stuffed animals because they like to hear it too. And we feel very safe.

Betsi

When he comes home late he comes into my room and stands there for a while looking at me Somtimes I pretend I'm asleep. Then he pulls up the blanket and kisses me on my head.

Kevin

Even if I'm bad my dad has to still like me because I am in his family. I think it's a law.

Alison

When I swing in the park my dad pushes me so I go up to the sky. I wish he would do it forever because it's the best thing of anything.

Jeremy

I saw my dad in his naked clothes. It was very interesting.
Natalie

Once when my dad was coaching little league there pitcher hit our batter and there was almost a fight. But my dad said there's a new rule — you're not allowed to smile. That made the guys really crack up.

Mark

When me and my dad play
tickle monster sometimes he
laughs so hard it feels like
the house will fall down.

Toni

HA   HA   HA

When me and my dad walk our dog I tell him what's bugging me. He listens very good but I wish he'd come to school with me. Then Jimmy Ryan couldn't bug me!

Ralph

When we were playing
freeze tag I farted —
and my Dad said
" You're OUT, that's a
move! " And we all
laughed our heads off.

Maxine

When my bowling ball goes in the gutter and I get mad my dad says I will love you even if it goes out the door and into the river. That's really silly but it's nice to know anyway.

Chad

There are two kinds of dads. Mean or Nice. I'm lucky because I have the nice kind.

~Trish

When I say "I'm bored" my dad says, "No you're not, you're Annie". When I fall down, my dad makes me tell the sidewalk I'm sorry. When my dad sees chocolate he goes CRAZY!

Annie

When he takes a nap no matter
how much noise you make he
just groans and keeps sleeping.
If you ask him a question you
might as well ask a wall.
Nothing could wake him not
even an ~~earth~~ earthquake.

Sam

My dad fell on the ice and cut his hand. He didn't cry. But I did. Then he made me feel better—which is one of the things dads are supposed to do.

Felice

When my father pays the bills he says "Darn it. Everything is getting more expensive these days!" I guess you have to be rich to be a father.

Denis

The greatest thing my
Dad does is he makes
money for our family.
He's pretty good at
it too!   Mikey

He doesn't play video games very good.
But he does it with me anyway when I
feel sad. Then I feel better and he feels
sad because I wipe him out every time.
Jesse

I can talk with him about a lot of things I can't talk with my mom about. But I'm not going to write it down because we'd get in trouble.

sanford

My father always asks were you a good boy today. But I think he already knows because he only asks when I'm already in trouble.

Louis

Sometimes we sing camp songs in the car and my dad does harmony. It's still the same songs but they make me feel nice.

orlando

He always tells me I can do anything if I stick with it and really try. What if I try to walk up the outside of the Umpire State Building?

Naomi

ROOM FOR IMPROVEMENT

My dad does things like make the beds and clear the table but he never never ever cleans the cat box! He says he comes from royal blood so he doesn't have to do litter boxes.

Steven M.

When I'm a father and my kids ask me why they can't stay up late I'll never tell them "because I said so."

Eric

My dad shows me how to draw. He says all you have to do is think a thought and then draw a line around it. He says it's easy but that's because he thinks I'm a genious.

    Willis

whenever you ask
him a question he
can go on and on
until you could just
die. But there are
many good things
about him too.
Bruce

My dad always tries to let me win when we play games because he doesn't want me to feel busted. But it's no fun to win if it's just because he's acting like a dumb dad.

Marty

I love when he tells jokes but I don't like when he does it to cheer me up. It doesn't work because when I'm sad I want to be alone.

Mollie

My dad and me love to make
a big mess when we cook
Pancakes on sunday. My mom
Says we are more trouble than
20 childfen!

   Max

One time we made this bet. Then he didn't give me the dime because he said he was just kidding. If I was his dad and he was the kid I wouldn't let him watch T.V. until he paid me.

Nathaniel

I never ask my dad about math because he said it gives him a bellyache. So my mom helps me. But he's very good at Civil War.

Nan

Whenever I ask my dad
"Do you know what
time it is?" he looks
at his wrist and says
"2 hairs past a freckle."
Which is sooooooooo
not funny it's pathetic!

Amy

My dad is very strict. That means you better not do what you're not s'pose to. And never do it again either.

Leonard

I love him very much. If he will raise my allowance I will love him even more.

Seth

My dad built a tree house
for me and my sister. We have
a sign that says KEEP OUT!
But he climbs up all the time
anyway. Sometimes it's fun
but not that much fun.
Keith

Every time we shoot a video he dances all around and makes these wierd faces. You'd never know in real life he's just this normal boring dad.

Alvin

He always thinks he's right. Even if you look it up and show him he's wrong, he like totally cannot admit it. He'd be much better if he wasn't so Dad-ish

Hallie

When he helps me with stuff from school he doesn't listen. If I say what does something mean, instead of just telling me he does the whole problem. And he does it his own way, not the way we were told in school.

Samantha B.

Whenever you ✎ catch him that he broke a promise he always says in his dad voice, "I didn't break a promise, I changed my mind." Yeah right.

Patricia

I Don't like when he eats off my plate when I'm not done with supper. But mostly he's a nice father.

Julie

I hate when my room is messy but I know where everything is and my dad barges in and makes me clean it up.

Anna

He yells when I use his tools and don't put them back. He could just tell me and I'd do it. But it's O.K. because he's always nicer after he talks grouchy.

Ned

He tries to calm me down when I'm really upset. Like when they go out and my brothers are mean to me. He tells me to just ignore them. But it doesn't work if you're not their father.

Lila

He's a really great dad except when he doesn't come out of the bathroom when I really have to go!

Norman

UNQUALIFIED
ENDORSEMENTS

When you have a nite mare and a monster is chasing you but you can't run fast enough my dad's the only one who knows just what to tell you to make it go away.

Ann-Marie

My dad's really neat.
When somebody comes
for a sleepover he
doesn't disapear in
his room and ignore us.
Christina

If Something Gets Broken my
mom Gets really really upset.
But my Dad's pretty loose about
stuff, He's Definitely MY
HERO.
Alicia

My dad has to be in a wheelchair but he can do most everything. Except walk and play sports. But I wouldn't trade him for anybody, even Mark McGwire!

Paul

He told me that when he was in the room at the hospitl while I was being born he sang a song because he was so happy that I came in the world. I'm going to do that when I'm a dad too.

Ernie

I love when he told me about what hapend before he became a teacher. His dad really wanted him to be a shoe salesman like him but my dad went to college. When I think of that I know how strong he is.

Megan

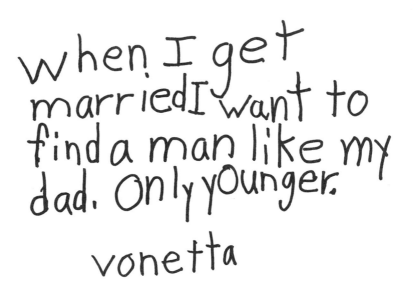

When I get married I want to find a man like my dad. Only younger.

vonetta

What I like best about my dad is that he doesn't treat me like a baby anymore.

Karla

I love my Dad because he's my only father and I have lived with him for all of my life. Also he's going to take me to see Godzilla.

Ross

MY dad CoUld BEAT UP
ANYBODY. He DOESN'T
ever do it BECAUSE he's
VeRY GENTLE.
BUT I JUST KNOW
He COULD.

MAX

Nobody laughs as loud as my dad. When he does it on the phone you can hear him all over the house. It's very happy.

Philippe

My father made up This
Song For my BiRThdAY.
It goes like YANKee DooDle.
"FREDDY BARLOW JusT
TURNED 10.
He's NEVER BEEN a BOTHER
He is The BEST KiD EVER BORN
I KNOW CAUse I'M His FATHER"
FrEDDY B.

One time when my teacher made
me stay after class he came and
told her she couldn't because he
had to take me to my violin lesson.
He's not afraid of anybody!

Carmella

Once this kid in my class copied from another kid's paper. I asked my Dad if I should tell on him. He said it would probly be best to mind my own business. Dads are good for problems like that.

Jake

When I'm in church sitting next to my dad it's one of the best times in life. I wish we could do it everyday instead of just on Sundays.

Lisbeth

My dad is the best dad
in the whole universe!
Sarah